T0196179

THE FARMER'S DAUGHTER'S GUIDE
TO NUTRITIOUS AND DELICIOUS EATING

Best Food, Recipes, and Advice—Even Your Mother Would Agree!

ROSANNE C. MARTINO

BALBOA
PRESS

A DIVISION OF HAY HOUSE

Copyright © 2017 Rosanne C. Martino.

All rights reserved. No part of this book may be used or reproduced by any means, graphic, electronic, or mechanical, including photocopying, recording, taping or by any information storage retrieval system without the written permission of the author except in the case of brief quotations embodied in critical articles and reviews.

Balboa Press books may be ordered through booksellers or by contacting:

Balboa Press
A Division of Hay House
1663 Liberty Drive
Bloomington, IN 47403
www.balboapress.com
1 (877) 407-4847

Because of the dynamic nature of the Internet, any web addresses or links contained in this book may have changed since publication and may no longer be valid. The views expressed in this work are solely those of the author and do not necessarily reflect the views of the publisher, and the publisher hereby disclaims any responsibility for them.

The author of this book does not dispense medical advice or prescribe the use of any technique as a form of treatment for physical, emotional, or medical problems without the advice of a physician, either directly or indirectly. The intent of the author is only to offer information of a general nature to help you in your quest for emotional and spiritual well-being. In the event you use any of the information in this book for yourself, which is your constitutional right, the author and the publisher assume no responsibility for your actions.

Any people depicted in stock imagery provided by Thinkstock are models, and such images are being used for illustrative purposes only. Certain stock imagery © Thinkstock.

Print information available on the last page.

ISBN: 978-1-5043-7741-6 (sc)
ISBN: 978-1-5043-7742-3 (e)

Library of Congress Control Number: 2017905538

Balboa Press rev. date: 04/13/2017

Contents

Introduction

The Best Food, Recipes, and Advice—Even Your Mother Would Agree!

The idea to write a book came to me after an evening of preparing a meal for some friends. I enjoy cooking for others and find that most of the time everyone wants Italian food. Halfway through dinner, I was already getting requests for another sumptuous event. A thought came to me to try to recreate the meal and write down the recipe. We do not usually cook with recipes in my family, so that was a novel idea. After that, when cooking, if a dish was exceptionally tasty and looked pretty, I would try to recreate it. I paid special attention in preparing delicious as well as nutritious foods, in not only Italian dishes but also my individual tastes, and I had to share them. Learning at a young age about how food was grown, harvested, and prepared, combined with my degree in holistic nutrition, I realized the amount of information in my head was overpowering. So I decided to write a book.

I hope you also enjoy my tribute to my family and my very fortunate life, including the Martino family photos. Consider this my contribution to your journey for good, healthy, and fun eating!

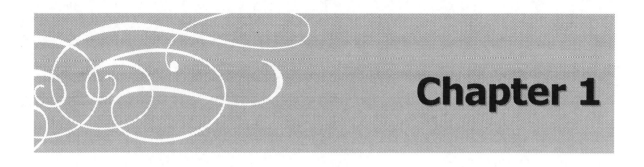

Chapter 1

My Life

Tell me what you eat, and I will tell you who you are.
—Jean Anthelme Brillat-Savarin

This book is a little of what I know about growing, preparing, sharing, eating, and enjoying homemade, delectable, and memorable meals that are actually good for you and good for the soul. I will help you not only prepare food but also know why you are eating it, besides the obvious, and give you some pointers on the spices, oils, and techniques that make the dish.

I believe in mindfulness and that mindful eating is conscious eating, an even better experience. Think about your body and all the parts that will flourish and be well nourished with everything it needs and what you give it.

Yes, I use shortcuts in some recipes, but if you learn the art of preparing a meal, you will find many ways to eat well and know your way around the grocery stores and farm markets as well as the kitchen. I will share some of my travel experiences in this book as well, as they always bring me back to the wonderful food that new places and tastes bring, to help elevate even the most sophisticated palate.

Of course, I admit to being a full-blooded and full-bodied Sicilian woman who believes health and food go together like Italian pane and vino. I was born and raised in the country on a fruit and horse farm and learned very early that having a garden of fresh vegetables and eating fruit off the tree, as well as knowing how to prepare these nutritional foods, was essential to my life. By the end of this book, you will realize that whatever you put in your mouth to eat affects your health. Unfortunately, there are many other influences in our lives that contribute negatively to our health, but this is the one thing we alone can control.

Growing up in the country, my family had many businesses, one of which was our country market. I spent many a summer, weekend, and holiday there, working and learning. I watched my parents explaining the simple ways of preparing the beautiful fresh goods, as well as growing the lovely herbs and plants we had in our greenhouse, and I felt very fortunate.

Spring opened up the market with Mother's Day and Easter plants in our beautiful greenhouse. In the summer, we would have a pick-ur-own strawberry patch and all the freshest of fruits and vegetables. Flowers covered the front of the market.

However, my favorite time of year was autumn: apple-picking time, a chill in the air, fresh raw cider, winter squash, pumpkins, and beautiful winter chrysanthemums lining the walkways. It was a busy time, as we were in two places at once. Thanksgiving was a joyous and grateful time, as harvest was over and Christmas on its way. My mother would always have a cornucopia on the table with fresh fruit and flowers of the season. Our horn of plenty was duly noted at our table.

At the end of the year, my father would reopen the market for a few short weeks to sell some of our beautiful Christmas trees, which was our customers' last visit for the year.

My first interest after high school was in health care. I worked in a hospital for a few years after college and then decided to start my own small business. I had many years working in the family businesses, dealing with the public and learning a lot, and decided to open a jean shop. What a great experience that was for my twenties! My 1957 Wurlitzer jukebox with all the flashing lights played endless rock 'n' roll for my customers. That was a great addition to their experience of shopping for funky blue jeans and their favorite rock band T-shirts.

After that, I moved to Florida and realized my passion was to help others in health care, and I learned much more working in the medical field. I ultimately broadened my career in the legal forum, using my medical knowledge as a successful tool. After many years of living and eating healthier, my interest in holistic medicine was evident. I finally received my bachelor's in holistic nutrition, became certified as a life coach, and realized at that time I had a lot of information that I needed to share. I found that many people avoid natural medicine and eating healthier for the simple reason they have not been exposed to or educated to understand it.

I will try to give you a healthy foundation, as well as some of my personal experiences, for the overall picture that I wish to paint for your complete experience of the *Farmer's Daughter's* book.

Buon appetito e la dolce vita!

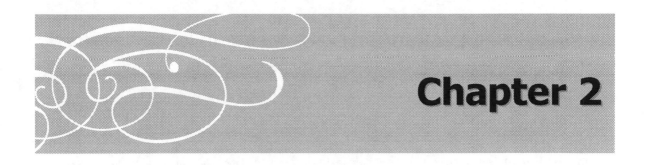

Chapter 2

The Pyramid

Our lives are not in the lap of the Gods, but in the lap of our cooks.
—Lin Yutang

If you are reading this book, by now you should have some idea of the different food groups to eat daily. This basically includes proteins, vegetables/fruits, dairy, grains, and fats.

I believe the largest part of the diet should be fresh food, mostly vegetarian based and colorful, and the least part animal protein and fats. First of all, processed foods have a limited use in my kitchen. Once you learn how to prepare these easy recipes, you will no longer want to put preservative-laden foods such as boxed potatoes and canned pastas into your body.

The food pyramid has changed over the years, and I believe for the better. A basic outline suggested is as follows: at the top, fats, oils, and sweets. Try to consume less than 30 percent or fifty grams per day of these. No matter what anyone says, you do need fats in your diet. But the problem is that not everyone knows the difference between good and bad fats. Everyone needs to tailor their fat consumption to their individual needs, so remember this is just a guideline.

Next on the list are dairy, yogurt, and cheese. This is a tough group for me, as I love mozzarella, ricotta, and feta. But two to three servings of dairy per day can't hurt. Yogurt can help your gut, for instance. Some people are lactose intolerant, but there are many items today that help with that.

Meat, fish, eggs, beans, and nuts are your proteins. You need them for muscle mass. You want to be strong and able to carry your bones around. Eat at least two to three servings a day and stay on the leaner side of animal protein. I prefer fish and find that I can get good fats and protein in salmon.

Vegetables and fruits are so important. I can eat every kind I know, and I love to mix them up with pasta, of course. I could drizzle delicious olive oil over any vegetable on earth. Eat at least three to five servings of vegetables per day, and you will feel so good.

Fruits do have sugar, so some people may eat fewer than two to four servings per day. Remember that the vitamins and antioxidants are really the reason to eat fruits.

On the bottom is the largest part of the pyramid, which contains breads, whole grains, rice, and pasta. We know where we stand on this—who could live without pasta and bread? The suggested number of servings is six to eleven per day. Carbohydrates can be a difficult item for many to control though. They do give you energy and fiber, so I do not suggest eliminating them completely.

The pyramid today includes one more item: water. Yes, you absolutely do need to drink water. Why on earth do some people perceive this as a bad thing? It is the elixir of life, and without it nothing will grow, function, or last for long. I am not including some additive to fool you into believing you are not drinking water—just water.

Chapter 3

Spices and Herbs

*Once you get a spice in your kitchen, you have it forever.
Women never throw out spices. Egyptians were buried with
them. I know which one I'm taking with me when I go.*
—Erma Bombeck

A Good Start: Spices and Herbs

In my opinion, just about anything you put in your mouth should taste good, and it will if you know how to properly season it. However, there is no rhyme or reason for pork rinds, but that is another issue.

If you have ever found yourself wandering hypnotically through a spice market, you will likely agree with me. The colors, aromas, and textures of rows and rows of beautiful, pungent spices bathe the senses, and one can immediately imagine the flavors in another delicious recipe.

One experience in particular comes to mind—when I traveled to the islands of Fiji, a magical part of the Pacific. Our driver took us to the market. It was a most exciting and unbelievable experience. The spices were so fresh and the colors so vibrant, I just wanted to take everything home with me. The fresh fish right out of the Pacific and of course kava root, was in great abundance.

Kava was a most interesting drink. In the Pacific islands, the natives consume kava daily. Instead of coffee breaks at work, they have kava breaks. The nightly kava ceremony for happy hour was an interesting event, one of which I took part in religiously. Before the horror of 9/11, bringing back bags of spices was a possibility, and it was so rewarding to return home with great treasures from abroad.

I believe in trying new things, and travel encourages one to be more adventurous. Those tastes just have to be recreated in your home kitchen. Herbs are so easy to grow too. Even if you have only one window box, you can still enjoy fresh spices. Remember, variety is the spice of life.

Garlic: Who does not like garlic? It not only is one of the most flavorful spices, but it also can act as an antibacterial. It has been known to even aid with earaches. As far as I'm concerned, anything that promotes a healthy immune system has to be good. Of course, let us not forget one reason most Italian foods are so delicious. Bake it, sauté it, roast it—just eat it.

Basil: Basil is wonderful. You can use it in food as well as beverages, including teas. Holy basil is known for its medicinal value and makes a great tea. This herb has great effects on digestion and can be another green in your salad.

Basil is easy to grow. One little plant can offer so many great flavors. Just remember to pinch off the white blooms, and it will grow forever. Basil also is a must in Sunday's pasta sauce. My mother, Rose, never would have a garden without lots of basil, parsley, oregano, and of course tomatoes.

Cinnamon: Yum. Warm spiced cider, tea, and hot cocoa come to mind. This stimulating and warming herb can be used for various gastrointestinal distress. It has a balancing effect on fruits and desserts. Also, a dash in your morning coffee is a great start to the day. A sprinkle in some warm milk to assist in a restful sleep can be comforting. This can also lower blood sugar and stimulate circulation.

Chives: How fun are they? Cut them up and sprinkle on scrambled eggs, tuna salad, mashed cauliflower, anything that a light onion flavor will enhance. I love them in salads. A cucumber and tomato with fennel salad is a refreshing appetizer.

Cumin: This is so great in curries. This gives eggplant a new twist when making a spread or pate. Cumin can help relieve gas or bloating. A very exotic flavor can come from this spice. This is most recognized in Indian dishes.

Fennel: Italians love *finocchio*, those big white bulbs that look like celery. Finocchio was always on the table at any holiday. I just love it for the refreshing anise flavor, and of course, it is also good for your digestion. Do not wait for a holiday to try this treat. Also, the green ends can be cut up and thrown into soup or over a salad.

Ginger: It is one of most versatile herbal stimulants. Ginger tea can be soothing for nausea or an upset stomach. As an oil, it can relieve muscle aches. I prefer my ginger in any Asian type dish I may try, adding a little heat to the recipe. I love ginger in any stir-fry, and it even makes a good cookie.

Rosemary: Chicken loves rosemary. When used as a shampoo rinse, it will invigorate your scalp and add shine to hair. Luckily, we brunettes benefit the most from this. Rosemary tea is known to relieve headaches.

Lavender: Ah, relax with this lovely scent. Any bedroom or bathroom is a haven for this purple flower. Of course, roasted lavender chicken with a little thyme cannot be forgotten as one of my favorite dishes. Aromatherapy was born with lavender in mind.

Mint: There are many varieties used for many things. I love fresh mint in ice tea with lemon, which can be cleansing and refreshing. Mint is very medicinal. We all know it helps bad breath, but it also acts as an aid for indigestion when taken as mint tea. I have a peppermint oil I keep handy for nausea or mild upset stomach. Just a whiff or two will quiet down the feeling.

Parsley: I put it in everything. Parsley is full of calcium, helps in digestion, and gives a great green color to all dishes. It is not just a garnish. Italian parsley with flat leaves is a slight variation from the curly parsley most commonly used. If you are juicing, add fresh parsley to a carrot, tomato, celery, apple juice, and your body will thank you.

Oregano: When making pasta sauce, do not forget the oregano. This peppery flavored spice in the marjoram family is delightful in meat dishes, meat pasta sauce, and vegetables. Also, it is easy to grow.

Pepper: I love pepper. I use white, black, red, fresh ground, flakes, any and all of it. If I am using curry for a spicy or Asian dish, I will hold the pepper. Sore throats do not like black pepper.

Salt: This is not a spice; it is a seasoning. It is listed here because most people think that salted food tastes better. It is a mineral. There are many different kinds of salt sold today, and some dissolve faster than others. Basically, there are sea salts and mined salt. Kosher salt dissolves faster, giving a saltier taste. Himalayan pink salt has many medicinal qualities. Personally, I do not use much salt in my food but find that elixirs and homeopathy include many varieties. These I do enjoy. I find that the exotic spices in my kitchen do the trick for tastier dishes without much need for salt. I never understood how people reach for the salt shaker before even tasting their food. We have about ten thousand taste buds on our tongue but only can detect five basic tastes. They are salty, sweet, bitter, sour, and umami. Umami is the newer one discovered and associated with glutamate, a nonessential amino acid. Umami means "delicious" in Japanese. Many people have to limit their intake of salt due to illnesses and limitations caused by salty fluid retention.

Tarragon: Once again, chicken has another reason for being dinner. Broiled chicken breasts sprayed with olive oil and sprinkled with tarragon are so basic but satisfying. Tarragon is also great in vinegars. It is more of a culinary herb than medicinal.

Thyme: Something else great for brunette hair. Also, it can be used as a disinfectant or toner for the skin. Parsley, sage, rosemary, and thyme are great for vegetables, meats, fowl, and soups.

Turmeric: From what I can tell, this may be one of the most important spices for health. I sprinkle a dash in everything. It may help in warding off just about anything, maybe even bad luck. It is golden and a staple in Indian dishes. It helps with circulation and menstrual cramps and can help in healing wounds. I love it and sprinkle it on my scrambled eggs for an even healthier breakfast. One caution would be if you are taking an anticoagulant medication; please be aware that it has an effect on clotting.

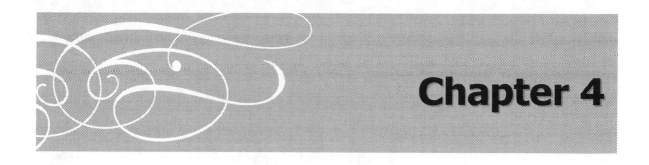

Chapter 4

Oils and Fats

A crust eaten in peace is better than a banquet eaten with anxiety.
—Aesop

Please, do not fear oils. Everyone you talk to has a different opinion about fats. In my opinion, you need some fat in your diet, or you will just shrivel, crack, and dry up. Your skin, hair, joints, and digestive tract, everything right down to your cells, need fats. There are many kinds of good fats that aide in vitamins A and D production. These are nuts, avocado, salmon, flax, and sesame seeds, to name a few. Of course, there are some bad ones. Stay away from the saturated and trans fats. As my father, Joe, often said in his teachings throughout my gifted childhood, "Moderation is a sign of refinement." I believe, knowing that, you can approach anything in your life and appreciate a little of everything, with some class.

Olive Oil: Virgin or extra-virgin only for my taste. This is a staple in the Mediterranean diet. Olive oil contains monounsaturated fat, which helps lower bad cholesterol. Due to olive oil's low smoke point, I do not recommend using it to cook with unless it is a quick sauté, to avoid smoking or burning. Salads and vegetables all love this oil. I recommend extra-virgin, double-pressed, Italian, or Spanish for flavors. I do not recommend buying it in bulk unless you are able to use it within three months. One memory of my travels to Italy includes the time I brought home a half gallon of wonderful oil from a beautiful medieval town in Tuscany called San Gimignano. Walking through the airport in Milan with that in hand was quite a task.

Grape-Seed Oil: When you need an oil with a high smoke point, this excellent source of vitamin E and antioxidants will do. Grape-seed oil has a nutty, delicate flavor and works in stir-frying or even baking. I keep it in my refrigerator.

Coconut Oil: This does have some saturated fat but also antioxidant powers. The natives of the South Pacific who eat coconuts all the time cannot be wrong. It has a high smoke point and can be used for sautéing as well.

Almond Oil: It is one of the best massage oils and smells so good. Eat almonds. A handful a day is a great source of vitamins E and K. Almond oil has a high smoke point and is easy to cook with.

Sesame Oil: It is great for stir-frying. It can be used for massage also, as it is detoxifying. However, do not try this together. Sesame oil has a medium smoke point. One precaution is that this oil is high in omega-6, something to consider, as one must have a balance between the sixes and the threes. I suggest using it rarely.

Omega-3 Fats/Flax: It has been said that Hippocrates was aware of the benefits of flax and used flaxseed as one of the first medicines. Flaxseed every morning on oatmeal adds the nutty flavor and the omega-3s. Sprinkle it on yogurt for an extra healthy snack. You can either buy the seeds and grind them in a coffee grinder or buy the ground meal. Either way, this offers an anti-inflammatory and antioxidant benefit. Walnuts and salmon also have omega-3. I believe flax can assist in daily colon health.

Omega-9: Olive oil. It decreases heart disease and lowers the LDL cholesterol. This is the low-density number, and is the bad cholesterol.

Omega-5: Palm oil.

Omega-7: Macadamia nuts and anchovies. This lowers the bad LDL cholesterol and triglycerides in your blood levels. It can raise your good cholesterol HDL numbers.

Omega-6: Your body needs very little, as too much may cause inflammation. Vegetable oils, walnuts, and seeds are a good source.

Butter: Butter may have gotten a bad rap in the past. However, you cannot cook without it, especially when you are baking. We always had real butter in our home. Margarine was considered a fake food. My mother used butter in baking and cooking. Nothing is more delicious than a slice of her fresh baked bread right out of the oven, with a smear of real butter and sprinkled with fresh black pepper to bring you to your senses. Like most delicious things in life, moderation, please.

Chapter 5

Protein

You don't need a silver fork to eat good food.
—Paul Prudhomme

When most people think of protein, they think only of meat. For some, that may be the case. I prefer vegetable protein, soybeans, tofu, eggs, some chicken, seafood, or a turkey burger occasionally. I stopped eating all other animal protein when I studied holistic nutrition. I realized I felt better eliminating that from my diet, and my body did not need it. I have never been anemic, so I know that there are other ways to incorporate iron and protein into your diet. Of note, vitamin B12 is found naturally in animal products, so you may need a supplement if you are a vegetarian. Proteins are about 20 percent of the body and are composed of amino acids. We need twenty-one amino acids to function properly and can only produce eleven of them ourselves. Not all foods have all essential amino acids, so it is a great idea to eat two or more together. There are lots of vegetarian sources for protein. I love beans, broccoli, spinach, lentils, many greens, brussels sprouts, and hummus. These are delicious sources. My mother, Rose, made the best lentil soup. Lentils are filled with iron. She would add escarole, carrots, and celery. Sometimes she would put a ham bone to give it just a little different flavor. It was excellent as a complete meal with some tiny pasta added and sprinkled with Parmigiano cheese. A slice of Italian bread with that on a cold winter's night was very welcomed in our home. If you are wondering, yes, pasta can be found just about everywhere in this book.

Cannellini beans, kidney beans, and garbanzo beans are all easy to incorporate in recipes. These are an alternative source of good, healthy protein and fiber and if cooked correctly should not have the gassy result that many people experience. Black beans are a staple in the Latin diet and with rice can be delicious. I love hummus too. Garbanzo or chickpeas are most common for hummus, but carrots, lentils, and edamame can be a tasty alternative.

Chapter 6

Seeds and Sprouts

*If you are what you eat, and you don't know what
you're eating, do you know who you are?*
—Claude Fischler

Seeds and nuts are the source of power in all vegetables, fruits, and grains. They can be used as a topping, added to dishes as a garnish, made into a spread, or eaten whole as a nutritious snack. These add sweetness, nutty flavor, protein, or good fats and minerals to your diet. Seeds such as hemp, flax, sesame, chia, sunflower, and pumpkin are high in protein, calcium, magnesium, iron, zinc, fiber, vitamin B1, and omegas. Amino acids in hemp seeds are an excellent protein. Chia seeds may help lower blood sugar. Do not waste your jack-o'-lantern pumpkin; easily scoop out the seeds and bake them. You will have a perfect snack.

Nuts such as walnuts, almonds, pecans, and cashews are my favorite and definitely have a power-packed nutritional effect. I prefer and suggest salt-free. Oatmeal without walnuts and flax meal is only 50 percent worth the effort to cook. Add your favorite milk and fruit, and this is fuel for the day. Also, your colon will appreciate this too. Nuts are a heart-healthy treat. They are high in omega-3 fatty acids, fiber, vitamin E, plant sterols to help lower cholesterol, and L-arginine, which is good for artery wall health. They should be eaten daily, so use your nutcracker. It is not just for Christmas.

Along with these very nutritionally necessary jewels, I like to include sprouts. Yes, the little green and white "complete plant" that we can eat before it grows up. Sprouts literally have all the nutrition that eating the fruit of the plant will offer. One concern only: please wash these thoroughly and purchase them from a reputable, safe environment.

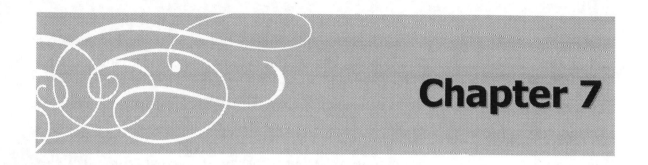

Chapter 7

Grains

What is food to one man is bitter poison to others.
—Lucretius

The whole grains, especially the low glycemic carbohydrate varieties, are the best choices. Most people eliminate these and many carbohydrates from their diet, thinking it is the best way to lose weight. I disagree. I believe they are necessary in your diet to keep your body functioning normally, without stress on your system. There are many misleading products for sale claiming whole grain ingredients that are not low glycemic. They can cause blood sugar levels to rise. The fiber in grains can assist in improving cholesterol levels and help in digestion. Examples of whole grains that I enjoy and have learned to use in many ways are: barley, millet, whole oats, brown rice, bulgur, farro, kasha, wild rice, spelt, and quinoa. These may need to be soaked and rinsed before cooking, and cook time usually is longer than most grains. My mother, Rose, made a hearty barley soup that was enjoyed in the winters in Upstate New York. She would add chicken and every vegetable possible to this soup.

I love farro, an ancient grain and a Mediterranean staple, as well as quinoa. I sometimes mix these with wild or brown rice. Being more creative, mushrooms, carrots, and beans can be mixed in for a fabulous side dish that is definitely filling. One of my favorite dishes is a Cornish hen roasted with brown sugar and cinnamon over carrots, mushrooms, and onions. Season with herbs d' Provence, or rosemary and tarragon. Add a side of one of these grains, and you have a most fulfilling and nutritious dinner.

Pasta is also in this section and, you may realize, is incorporated in my weekly recipes. There are many kinds, flavors, sizes, and shapes of this very popular carbohydrate. There are entire books written about pasta. I love to try spinach and artichoke pasta. These may have less carbs but do have gluten. There are gluten-free items on the market now, which is necessary for many diets. Many people feel that eating carbohydrates is a sin and completely eliminate them from the diet.

If eating fresh pasta has not been an experience for you, I suggest trying it. I can remember when my grandmother would decide to make fresh pasta on Sunday morning. We would lay out a clean white sheet on one of the beds. She would roll out the dough of durum wheat or semolina into spaghetti, cavatelli, fettuccine, ravioli, or tortellini, to name a few of my favorites. We would assist her in carrying the pasta to the sheet and lay it all out carefully to dry, just a little bit before cooking. Now, of course, there are machines to do most of the work, and wooden racks to hang the pasta on. Fresh pasta cooks quickly, so make sure everything else is ready to be served. Remember al dente is the only way to cook pasta.

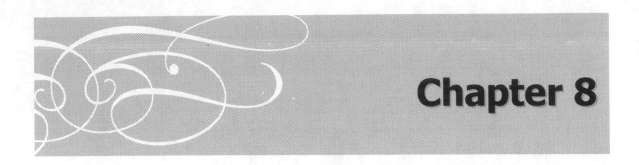

Chapter 8

Dairy

*If you really want to make a friend, go to someone's home and eat with
him ... the people who give you their food give you their heart.*
—Cesar Chavez

As a baby, I was told, I was allergic to milk, so I was given soymilk. Today, I am not
that fond of soymilk but will use it on my oatmeal, cereal, and in some cooking,
as well as in pancake mix. There are many kinds of milk on the market now, and
many are not dairy based. I like to try all the variations to see which suit me the best
nutritionally and how my body reacts to digesting them. Many people believe they
are lactose intolerant, so the nut milks are a good choice and can be tasty. There are
many options, but you should be mindful of the sugar content of the product.

Say cheese. Most everyone likes cheese. Even dogs love it. Give me a good piece of
well-aged Parmigiano Reggiano with a slice of prosciutto, and I can have a quick
and tasty snack. Italians love cheese. You can sprinkle it on everything. Shave it
over a fresh Caesar salad or pasta. A caprese salad is my favorite antipasto. Fresh
tomatoes, mozzarella, and basil drizzled with olive oil and balsamic vinegar, light
and sweet. Ricotta is a favorite on any pasta. I like cottage cheese with fruit on top
as a protein snack. Of course, if dairy does not cause you gastrointestinal distress,
eat it. Calcium found in dairy is so very important for bones and teeth.

Cheese has calories and fat. There are light and vegetable cheeses for those who
prefer alternatives. Cream cheese is another one many people avoid. However, if
you ever tried to eat lox and bagels without it, you knew something was missing.
Sour cream is almost sinful over fresh corn on the cob, sprinkled with black pepper.

I enjoy a light fresh fruit salad or Waldorf with crisp apples to create a refreshing summer side dish or dessert.

Yogurt is amazing for your body. I prefer Greek yogurt and try to stay within 1 to 2 percent fat, as it has less sugar. I find that many people feel they need the probiotic products. These can help many digestive disorders, but I believe they should only be used for a limited period of time. They give your body a chance to balance and readjust the digestive tract. However, you want your body to achieve balance on its own. These along with eating the healthy foods your cells need should allow you to achieve stasis among various forces in the body, as well as the beginning of healthy systemic functioning.

Chapter 9

Vegetables

*We may find in the long run that tinned food is a
deadlier weapon than the machine gun.*
—George Orwell

My absolute favorite foods and basis of my existence are fresh vegetables. In every meal, I will incorporate a vegetable if I can. That is why I love making omelets and frittatas, so that I can add everything from zucchini squash to peppers and mushrooms. If I feel I am not getting enough of these vitamins, or a little sluggish, I will make juices. Sometimes I use the pulp when juicing and add it to soups. I do not waste the water that greens are cooked in either. I will save it, chill it, and drink that as a supplement for the day. The nourishment of the real green vegetable juice is something I do not believe you can buy. It also is a good cleanser if you want to detox, or just drink it daily.

One of my favorites is the sweet potato. They have been known to help stabilize blood sugar levels and work as anti-inflammatories. Any potato is considered a starchy vegetable, but sweet ones are high in A, C, E, manganese, and of course fiber. Add a little cinnamon and enjoy. I try to eat greens every day. I am a believer in a very colorful meal. Nothing is prettier on the table than a multi-green salad, with hearts of palm, artichoke hearts, beets, cucumber, berries, walnuts, chia or pumpkin seeds, sweet mini peppers, cherry or grape tomatoes, and scallions or red onions. As a main course, add salmon, tuna, shrimp, or chicken. Top it off with some crumbled feta or blue cheese.

Cruciferous vegetables, including kale, cabbage, bok choy, endive, broccoli, and cauliflower, all are cancer-fighting champions. They reduce oxidative stress in your body and help the liver detoxify free radicals. Antioxidants are my favorite nutrient. Eating one to two cups a day is easy and should be a goal. I love to steam these and add pepper, olive oil, and lemon. There is one concern for some regarding kale and spinach, however. Remember they do pack a whopping amount of vitamin K, which assists in blood clotting. If you are taking anticoagulant medication, please consult your doctor. All the green leafy ones are so good. Just mix it up and even out the benefits of these greens.

I grew up eating Swiss chard. All the colors were in the garden. Other favorites are spinach, mustard and collard greens, kohlrabi, daikon, romaine lettuce, dandelion greens, and watercress just to name a few. Another memory brings me to when I was sent outside by my grandmother, Lena, or my mom, Rose, to walk our massive lawns on the farm armed with a small knife and a bowl. I was to cut the dandelion greens for a salad. They were easy to find, especially with the little yellow flower growing in the middle. However, I took much care to pick only the ones growing away from any duck or doggie walkways. Dandelion tea is a great liver detox. These greens are full of lutein for your eyes and antioxidants for the heart. I cook them and prepare them basically the same as the cruciferous vegetables. I am impressed that in the stores today you can actually find a bag of dandelion or watercress greens. These are a great addition to your regular salad for more color and vitamins.

If I can, I will use onions—red, sweet, scallions, or yellow—in anything. I love garlic. Garlic is not only a spice, antibacterial, anticlotting agent, and antiviral but also an anti-inflammatory. I will add garlic and onions to mostly anything I eat, including omelets. If bad breath is a concern, try mint, fennel, cloves, or anise-licorice flavor.

Health tip: garlic oil warmed on a cotton ball can help relieve an earache.

I am very fond of mushrooms and like to use them in many ways. I stuff large portobello mushrooms, bake them in the oven, and make believe I am eating a steak. Yes, the recipe is in this book. I love to make dishes with different varieties that add texture and taste. They are high in vitamins C and B, calcium, and minerals. They can support your immune system and reduce inflammation.

I cannot stress enough the importance of eating squash. There are so many varieties of this wonderful vegetable, which can be cooked in so many ways. I can make zucchini squash at least five different ways. We rarely ate potatoes in my family. My mother utilized the winter varieties of squash for baking and in soups. I remember my father, Joe, telling a story of one of our regular customers at the farm market. He was a gentleman who purchased large quantities of yellow and zucchini squash on a weekly basis. He shared his story with my father about his diagnosis of cancer and how he was advised to eat squash due to the healing properties of the vegetable. I can remember how my father was touched by his story and how our garden grew more abundantly.

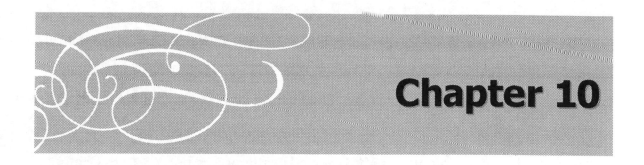

Chapter 10

Fruit

If music be the food of love, play on.
—William Shakespeare

I love fruit. Organic or not, I will eat just about anything that grows on trees. Of course, some vegetables can be considered fruits, but that is another chapter. Growing up on fruit farms was a beautiful and delicious existence. In the spring, beautiful apple blossoms, peach blossoms, and the sweet honey bees pollinating to their heart's desire was an actual event. It was a joyous and beautiful time to be outside. I waited for the beekeeper to come and leave his hives of hungry busy bees to pollinate our orchards. It was exciting to watch, and they were so busy you could walk among them without fear of being stung. I never could understand how most of them always were back to the hive in time to return home to make their honey and not be left behind. Every year, I looked forward to getting bottles of our apple blossom honey after they did their job. What a great lesson in the natural cycle of life.

My memories of the new foals being born and playing in the paddocks, feeding them hay and oats and apples, all come to mind. I will never forget a most unique memory in the spring when I was about eight years old. I wanted to feed one of my ponies and had to get into one of the very large feed bins in the barn. Our foreman, Harry, told me to look in the one bin by the door. As I raised the lid and peered over the side, to my surprise there lay a tiny white spotted fawn. I started yelling, and of course, Harry had just put the baby in there for me to find and came running around the corner. She was the most adorable pet and even though she was a wild deer, she needed our help. For the next few months, my mother, Rose, made bottles of milk and cereal for Bamba, along with bottles for my baby sister, Gina. Bamba seemed to take very well to us, especially our collie, Flame, who would be found curled up with the little deer in one of our horse stalls in the barn. We all took turns feeding our unique pet until she was able to fend for herself.

Of all fruits, I am partial to apples. An apple a day keeps the doctor away. I believe my father, Joe, ate an apple a day. He would have apples in every vehicle, on every trip, and even as gifts when visiting friends or relatives. A bag of our double red delicious apples was a sumptuous gift received by many. My mother, Rose's, famous apple strudel or pie was a heavenly addition to any meal or special occasion. Apples are high in antioxidants, and those red delicious are one of the highest. They are full of fiber, sugar, and pectin.

Health tip: An upset stomach always feels better after some thin, cold slices of apple to chew on. Pectin adds relief.

At the end of harvest, the last task was to pick up the apples that had dropped from the trees. They would be hauled off to the cider mill and pressed into delicious, fresh raw apple cider. We would sell it at our country market ice cold. It was also enjoyed served hot with cinnamon sticks to warm us in front of the fireplace after a day of skiing or on cool autumn nights. We did not waste anything on our farms. We would burn apple tree wood in our fireplaces in the winter, and a lovely aroma would permeate the room.

There are many excellent choices of fruit to obtain healthy amounts of antioxidants, including most berries: black, blue, cranberries, strawberries, and raspberries. Plums and cherries also. Cherry juice is known to aid in relieving arthritic symptoms. When I was a child, I remember my grandfather, Ignazio, would make fresh cherry juice by the gallon and sell it at his country market. Customers from New York City would come there every year, just for that special blend of fresh cherry juice. I remember his famous artwork posted around the store. He was a very creative artist and would sketch scenes from the newspapers, which were so unique. That may be where I inherited my need to paint, and color, and create.

One of my favorite homemade juice recipes is: six large cored apples, about one inch of fresh gingerroot, the juice of two lemons, and about one cup water. Run the apples and ginger through a juicer. Stir in citrus juice and water. I like this refreshing drink ice cold. It is very good for digestion.

Citrus fruit or juice is so important in the diet. When sailors would manifest scurvy on long ocean voyages, they just needed vitamin C. They realized having limes on board ships eliminated the problem. Some people tend to overdo the C supplement, which can be a waste of money. Your body will excrete it anyway. I suggest eating fruit or making your own juice, as many processed juices are just laden with added sugar. If you have digestive issues, find a way to incorporate the fruit into smoothies, on salads, or with fish or chicken. There are so many satisfying citrus dishes that can help you get your Cs.

Most people I see eat a banana a day, so they say. Bananas are the basis of most smoothies, which have now taken the place of many meals, when protein is added. Bananas are excellent for potassium, and if you have absolutely no time to prepare a meal, then eating one is a good idea. It even has its own bag. I prefer them on the greener side than too ripe. If they ripen too fast, then make banana bread.

I tend to enjoy many of the more exotic fruits, and living in a tropical region, I am able to find most anything grown in that variety. Mango, pomegranate, pineapple, coconut, star fruit, and passion fruit are worthy of any meal, dessert, or drink. I love fruit on salads when the temperature rises into the nineties. Anything in the summer or hot weather tastes better with a fruity accompaniment. If you have to watch your sugar intake, this may be a challenge, but remember, moderation. Remember to wash your fruit and vegetables well. I grew up able to pick off the tree and out of the garden, but not everyone has that opportunity, unless you are fortunate to have some space and you are growing your own.

Many people choose to eat only organic. I believe that certain fruits are healthier if eaten organic, but only because of the peeling option. I have no memories of washing an apple after I picked it from one of our trees. Rubbing it on your shirt to shine it up was all we did before enjoying that crispy, sweet fruit.

Chapter 11

Recipes

Everything you see, I owe to spaghetti.
—Sophia Loren

The following recipes are from: my kitchen, my mother, Rose's, kitchen, my maternal grandmother, Lena's, kitchen and my sister, Lorraine's, kitchen. Enjoy!

Ora di Colazione—Breakfast

I am a firm believer in eating breakfast. I never understood people who could start their day without any fuel for the fire. How can you go out and face the world running on empty? This brings to mind another one of my many warm memories when getting up for school. My father, Joe, first one up early, always made sure there was something on the table for our breakfast. He would have cereal, fruit, oatmeal, or a boiled egg with toast. We had a peach orchard on our farm too. There is no sweeter memory than those fresh-picked white or golden peaches that only my father grew on the top of our highest hill. If those were in our cereal, we knew we were special. My mother would make sure she canned many mason jars of those jewels to last our family over the winter months. We always made it to the table in enough time to start our day with a light nutritious breakfast, ready to face the world. To this day, I am a regular breakfast fan.

Oatmeal

3/4 cup old-fashion oats
dash cinnamon

2 teaspoons flax meal
1 tablespoon walnuts or pecans
1 tablespoon granola, if desired

Add water to cover all ingredients and cook one minute in microwave. (If using steel-cut oats, boil for 15–20 minutes.) Add coconut, soy, almond, or any milk of choice. Top off with choice of fresh berries, half a banana, peaches, or whatever is in season for the total antioxidant meal. Enjoy a hearty, healthy, and low-fat breakfast.

Greek Yogurt Starter

1/2–1 cup Greek yogurt, 1 percent fat
1 teaspoon ground flax meal
1 teaspoon walnuts or seeds
fresh fruit, preferably berries
1–2 tablespoons granola, if desired

I prefer Greek style yogurt, usually plain or vanilla. This is quick, refreshing, and good for your gut. This is a good snack also.

Omelet

1 whole egg
1/2 cup egg whites

Spinach, mushrooms, onions, small sweet pepper, any vegetable of choice, or bits of ham or bacon, if desired, mixed all together. A sprinkle of shredded cheese melts all flavors before folding.

Spray pan with butter or olive oil and add everything but eggs. Cook until softened and then add eggs. To flavor, add spices of your choice. Fold. I use more pepper than salt. Turmeric is the all-around, good-for-you spice, so sprinkle away. Add hot sauce or salsa on the side for a spicy flavor.

If desired, add your bread of choice—whole wheat, rye toast, toasted muffin, or bagel. Choose your toppings. Fresh fruit preserve with less sugar is great. Do not forget peanut butter. It has protein and fat, but limit to one tablespoon please. Real butter is best on any bread but not with the peanut butter.

Breakfast Sandwich of Champions

1 large brown egg, cage-free if possible
1–2 slices thin ham
1 slice skim mozzarella, provolone, or swiss cheese, your choice
1 teaspoon mayonnaise or Miracle Whip
1 small sandwich-size ciabatta roll
1–2 tomato slices
butter spray
dash of salt
pepper
turmeric
chives
fruit of choice

Spray pan with butter spray to coat, cook egg on both sides, and add ham slices to warm. Lightly toast roll, mostly to heat it through. Spread mayo on both sides of the roll. Begin layering: ham, egg, tomato, cheese, ham. Top and let melt together before cutting in half. Have a half a banana or orange to refresh the palate. You are good to go, especially if you miss lunch. This is a powerful, hearty, healthy, fast, delicious start to the day and includes protein, calcium, carbs, vegetables, fat, and vitamin A.

Sunday Frittata

4 eggs
2 egg equivalent whites
butter spray or olive oil
milk
1 zucchini squash
1 medium onion, chopped
2 slices ham, chopped
1 cup mozzarella or swiss cheese

In a large sauté pan, add oil or butter. Whisk together all eggs with a little milk. Add and slightly cook onions until wet. Add any vegetables to soften, then meat. Pour eggs over all ingredients and cook slowly on medium-low heat. Add spices, pepper, turmeric, parsley, and garlic if preferred. Sprinkle and add cheese of choice, one or two different kinds for best flavor. Cover and turn off heat. Let settle, and when cheese is melted, serve. If desired, choose crusty Italian bread, bagels, or biscuits, whatever is your favorite with eggs. This will feed at least three people.

One Soft-Boiled Fresh Brown Egg

1 fresh, large brown egg
1/2 banana or berries or peaches
toast with butter and/or fresh jam

Soft-boil egg, 2–3 minutes in small pot. Prepare side of fruit. Add your choice of bread for toast. Use real butter and real jam. This is what got me to school many mornings.

Raisin Challah French Toast

3 slices raisin Challah bread 1/2–1/4-inch thick
butter spray or coconut oil
1 egg
real maple syrup
butter or olive oil spread
powdered sugar

In frying pan, cover pan with spray or oil. Dip bread in whisked egg on both sides and place in medium heated pan. Brown both sides. Serve with syrup, a sprinkle of powdered sugar, and preferred spread. If desired, use a fruit spread instead of butter, but raisins bring sweetness, so I prefer the butter. A side of fresh fruit is a great accompaniment.

Fried Egg and Lox Sandwich

1 egg
2 slices walnut raisin bread

1 slice salmon lox
1 slice tomato
1 slice red onion, thin
cream cheese
butter spray

Lightly fry egg in butter spray, both sides, breaking yolk. Lightly toast bread and spread a thin layer of cream cheese. Build a sandwich with tomato, egg, lox, and onion. Lots of protein and omegas.

Spuntino—Snacks

Turkey Roll-Ups

sliced turkey or chicken breast
fennel, carrot, red or yellow pepper slices/sticks

Roll up everything in a slice of turkey or chicken breast. This is just enough to stop the hungry feeling.

Hummus and Salami Rolls

1/2 cup hummus, any kind
low-fat genoa salami slices
Provolone cheese slices, if desired

Spread slices with a smear of hummus and roll up. Great for an antipasto too.

Greek Yogurt Parfait

1 cup Greek yogurt of choice
fresh fruit
granola
walnuts
flax meal

Plain yogurt is usually best if adding fresh fruit. Add nuts and flax, and granola if a heartier snack is desired. This is very satisfying and refreshing.

Rice Cake Cookie

1 flavored or plain large rice cake
1 tablespoon of Nutella, almond butter, or peanut butter

Spread cake with choice of butter, and your sweet tooth will be pleasantly surprised. Lots of energy too.

Smoked Nova Salmon Nosh

3 slices or strips nova salmon
2 tablespoons cream cheese with chives or Greek cream cheese
2 slices red onion
1/4 teaspoon capers
2 cherry tomatoes halved
flat bread crackers, rice crackers, or no crackers

Layer all ingredients, roll up or on cracker. Add a cherry tomato, some capers, and you have a perfect protein-filled, tasty snack.

Prosciutto Sticks

1 package of crisp bread sticks
1/2 pound ricotta cheese
1/2 pound prosciutto, thinly sliced
1/2 pound assorted Sicilian or Greek olives

Wrap a slice of prosciutto around top half of breadstick. Dip it in ricotta to cover at least one inch. Enjoy with some Italian olives. Yes, you can double-dip this easy antipasto.

Hot Spinach Artichoke Dip

4 cups spinach chopped

14 ounces artichoke hearts, chopped and drained

1 cup fresh tomatoes diced

1/2 cup onion chopped

1 clove garlic minced

1/2 cup shredded mozzarella cheese

1/2 cup shredded swiss cheese

1/3 cup grated Parmigiano cheese

1 cup Miracle Whip

1 cup Caesar dressing

1/3 cup sour cream

1/2 tablespoon hot pepper sauce

Mix all ingredients in large baking dish. Bake 40–45 minutes at 350 degrees F, or until lightly browned. Serve with assorted crackers. I prefer unflavored wheat or rice crackers, as the dip is very flavorful. This is a famous appetizer of mine.

Ora di Pranzo—Lunch

Chicken Salad with a Twist

1 large can white meat chicken, drained

2 tablespoons plain Greek yogurt

2 tablespoons mayonnaise or Miracle Whip

3–4 tablespoons Caesar dressing

1 cup sweet peas

1/4 cup sweet or red onion chopped

1/2 cup hearts of palm cut into small pieces (not too small or you have mush)

dash garlic powder

pepper to taste

1 tablespoon sweet relish

Mix all ingredients in large bowl. If sandwich is your choice, ciabatta rolls, onion rolls, or bread of the day. Add romaine lettuce and one to two slices of swiss or Munster cheese. Enjoy with some vegetable sticks or dehydrated green beans for that crunchy taste. This can also be served over a bed of mixed greens with raisins, cranberries, and a vinaigrette.

Red, White, and Green Salad

1 can red beets or yellow beets, quartered and drained
1 cup fresh green beans cooked or raw cut in half
1 cup romaine or Bibb lettuce
1/4 cup fresh fennel, cut up
1/4 cup goat cheese
1 tablespoon walnuts, chopped
2 tablespoons olive oil
3 tablespoons balsamic vinegar or champagne vinegar
pinch salt
pepper
turmeric
parsley

Cut up all vegetables in bite-size pieces and mix together. Option of red onion to this salad is a savory addition.

Lite Tuna Mixed Salad

1–2 cups romaine lettuce, chopped
1–2 cups arugula
1/2 cup green or red cabbage, chopped
1/4 cup red onion, sliced
1 small cucumber sliced, no need to peel
cherry tomatoes or plum, halved
small sweet pepper or roasted pepper, sliced
1 can or envelope yellow fin tuna in olive oil or Tonno Italian tuna, drained
1/4 cup shredded cheddar or mozzarella
strawberries or blueberries, halved

balsamic dressing (olive oil, parsley flakes, garlic powder, basil chopped, lemon juice, and balsamic vinegar)

Dressing:

1/4 cup olive oil
1/4 cup balsamic vinegar
salt
pepper
1/2 lemon juice
1 teaspoon basil, chopped
1 teaspoon parsley, chopped
1/4 teaspoon garlic powder

In large bowl, mix greens and all vegetables. Top with tuna, fruit, and cheese. Toss with balsamic dressing. Perfect alfresco lunch. Serve with crackers or breadsticks.

Turkey Mushroom Burger

4-ounce turkey burger
3 mushrooms, sliced
1 small onion, sliced
Provolone or swiss cheese, sliced
roll of choice, ciabatta, sandwich, sourdough
olive oil
a pinch of each salt, pepper and garlic powder

Heat pan with oil and brown burger on one side for good sear. Add vegetables and flip burger. Cook to taste. Add salt, pepper, garlic powder. On warm bread, add avocado, ketchup, or choice of spread. Layer all ingredients and top with cheese to melt. Serve with chips or sweet potato fries.

Antipasto—Appetizer

Party Antipasto

Find a large platter and cover entire space with lettuce leaves. Layer all ingredients, rolling up meat slices and so on. My favorite ingredients are listed below. I find that this is a creative event, so use as much as can fit on the platter. I hardly ever have leftovers. A sparkling glass of cava or prosecco vino for the cocktail hour is a necessary accompaniment.

cured meats (Genoa salami, capicola, mortadella, and prosciutto)
fresh small mozzarella balls marinated in olive oil and basil
fresh provolone and/or Parmigiano, cut up in chunks
marinated artichoke hearts
cherry tomatoes
fennel sticks and carrot sticks
marinated green and black olives
Sicilian green olives with red pepper flakes in olive oil
roasted red peppers

Serve with slices of crusty Italian bread and breadsticks.

Sicilian Polipo Antipasto

1 fresh, small or medium-size octopus
extra-virgin olive oil
juice of 2–3 lemons
2 cloves garlic, chopped
fresh mint leaves
parsley
salt
pepper
fresh Italian bread, if desired, to soak up the juice

In large pot, boil on medium whole octopus for about 5–10 minutes. When able to pierce skin, add salt and remove from heat. Cut up all tender parts into bite-size pieces. Remove excess skin. In bowl, add all other ingredients. Add the octopus pieces. Mix well and chill if desired. My family loved to eat this while warm, as the flavors just melted together for a delightful beginning to our Christmas Eve tradition of the "Seven Fishes."

Ora di Cena—Dinner

Linguini with Vongole Sauce

2 dozen fresh clams
1 pound linguini pasta
1 cup clam juice
2 cans of baby clams
1 cup water
Italian parsley
lemon juice of 2 lemons
2 garlic cloves, minced
1 small onion, chopped
2 tablespoons olive oil
Pinch of salt and pepper

In saucepan, sauté onion, parsley, and garlic in olive oil. Add clam juice, salt, pepper, and well-scrubbed clams. In medium pot, cook pasta. Remove whole clams opened, from pot, and set aside. Add pasta to clam sauce. Add a little drizzle olive oil. Top with whole clams. Line dish with clams in shells. Sprinkle fresh Parmigiano Reggiano cheese and fresh parsley. Sometimes I add steamed mussels as an alternative to additional clams. Hint: for a quick fix on Friday night, canned white wine clam sauce is delicious.

Chicken and Kale, Peas, Squash over Pasta

4 boneless skinless chicken breasts
1 medium onion, chopped
5 cloves garlic, minced
1 can peas
3–4 yellow squash peeled, chopped into 1-inch pieces
4–6 cups fresh kale, stems removed
1/2–1 pound small penne or small ravioli
shredded mozzarella cheese
grated Parmigiano Reggiano cheese

1/2 cup pesto
basil
parsley
salt
pepper to taste
2 tablespoons olive, grape-seed, or coconut oil

This dish can be a wonderful meal for guests but a great Sunday dinner for anyone. In large saucepan, sauté chicken breasts until brown on both sides. Add squash, garlic, and onion. Add spices to taste. Lower heat to simmer with one can of peas; do not drain. If desired, a bag of frozen peas will do as well. Add kale cut up into smaller pieces and cook until wilted. Top with shredded mozzarella and cover. Remove from heat. Drain pasta. In large pasta bowl, lightly mix pasta with pesto and top with chicken and vegetables. Garnish with grated cheese and fresh basil or parsley. This is a great leftover for lunch any day of the week.

Chicken and Kidney Beans

4 boneless skinless chicken breasts
3 carrots cut bite size
1 onion, chopped
4 cloves garlic, minced
3–4 cups greens (spinach or escarole)
1 can red kidney beans
turmeric
salt
pepper
tarragon
parsley
basil
herbs de Provence
3 tablespoons grape-seed oil
1/2 cup shredded mozzarella
brown rice/quinoa or farro
1/2 cup water or chicken or vegetable stock

In large skillet, brown chicken in oil. Add onion, garlic, carrots and cook until softened. Add can of beans; do not drain. Add water or chicken or vegetable stock. Add greens last, just to soften. Season, cover, simmer on low-medium until chicken is cooked tender, at least 20 minutes. Sprinkle with shredded cheese, remove from heat, and cover. Let rest for a few minutes. Scoop over choice of grain. This was a favorite of my family over penne pasta.

Tropical Orange Chicken

4 skinless boneless chicken breasts
1–2 tablespoons olive/vegetable oil
Pinch of salt and pepper
1 teaspoon sugar
1/2 cup orange marmalade
1/2 cup orange juice

In large nonstick skillet or saucepan, brown chicken over medium heat on both sides. Reduce heat and add mixture of sugar, marmalade, juice, and salt and pepper. Simmer covered about 15 minutes until chicken is cooked through. Serve over wild rice. Add a side of asparagus or any greens to complete the dinner.

"Pasta" Primavera

2 yellow or zucchini squash, peeled
1/2 cup sundried tomatoes, soaked to soften
3 tablespoons olive oil
1 tomato, chopped
1/2 cup black Greek or Italian olives, pitted
1/4 cup chopped fresh basil
1/4 cup chopped fresh parsley
1/4 cup pine nuts
salt
white pepper

Slice squash into long, thin noodles. Set aside. Combine all other ingredients in food processor or blender just to blend, not puree. This recipe may be heated and the squash lightly boiled to resemble spaghetti. Some may prefer this as a cold dish. Toss the sauce with noodles and serve. If desired, add some grated cheese to top off the flavors.

Eggplant Parmigiano

2 eggplants, peeled and cut into 1/4–1/2-inch slices
2 eggs
2–3 cups Italian bread crumbs
Parmigiano cheese
2 cans large crushed tomatoes sauce or 2 jars of favorite red sauce
1-2 cups mozzarella cheese, sliced or shredded
olive oil and/or grape-seed oil or coconut oil for higher smoke value
garlic powder
basil
salt
pepper
2 tablespoons milk

Beat eggs with a splash of milk. Dip slices of eggplant into egg mixture and then into bread crumbs. Have skillet heating with grape-seed oil, or coconut or olive oil. Lightly brown on both sides over medium heat. In glass or nonstick pan, layer eggplant, sauce, spices, and cheese. Top with additional cheese and bake in oven at 350 degrees F for at least 30 minutes to let everything melt together. Remove and let rest before cutting. Serve with side of pasta or choice of chicken or steak. Leftover eggplant is great on a sandwich with a slice of provolone, ham, or salami.

Eggplant Rollatini

2–3 eggplants, peeled and cut lengthwise into 1/4-inch slices
2 eggs beaten with a splash of milk
2 cups Italian bread crumbs
1/4 cup grape-seed oil
2 1/2 cups ricotta cheese

2 large cans crushed tomato sauce as below or 2 jars of favorite red sauce
5 cups shredded mozzarella

Prepare eggplant as Parmigiano recipe. Preheat oven to 350 degrees F. In large baking dish, pour sauce to cover bottom. Place slices of eggplant in pan, lining each slice with ricotta. If desired, you can add a slice of prosciutto on top. Roll up each slice tightly and place seam down. Pour additional sauce over rolls and top with shredded cheese. Bake for 45 minutes until lightly browned and cheese is melted. If desired, serve over angel hair pasta. A very light and delicious Sicilian version of an eggplant main course.

Baked Stuffed Portobello Mushroom

2 large portobello mushrooms
1 cup Italian bread crumbs
1/2 cup grated cheese
1/4 cup mascarpone or Asiago cheese
2 cloves garlic, minced
2 tablespoons parsley
Pinch salt and pepper
2 tablespoons olive oil

Rinse lightly or brush mushrooms. Clean out inside of cap. Mix all ingredients together and fill each cap to top. Spray with olive oil and sprinkle a little Parmigiano on top. Bake in oven on lightly greased cookie sheet for 25–30 minutes at 350 degrees F until tender and lightly browned. These can be a main course or a side. If you prefer, add some Italian sausage or turkey sausage to the filling for a hearty dish.

Vegetable Bake

1 eggplant, sliced, partially peeled
2 zucchini squash, sliced, not peeled
2 cups broccoli, cut up in small pieces
1 cup kale, stems removed
1 medium sweet onion, chopped
4 cloves garlic, minced

3 tablespoons olive oil
tomato sauce (1–2 jars or fresh made)
2 cups ricotta cheese
basil
salt
pepper
parsley
1 cup grated Parmigiano or Romano cheese
2 cups sliced or shredded mozzarella cheese

In large baking or lasagna pan, spread olive oil over bottom. Begin layers of ingredients with eggplant. Alternate vegetables, spices, cheese, and sauce. Top with mozzarella and grated cheese. Bake at 375 degrees F for 30–40 minutes. Variations could include cannelloni beans throughout layers. Remove and let set covered. Cut like lasagna and serve. This also is delicious on a sandwich or as a vegetable burger.

The Best Italian Meatballs

2 pounds ground chuck and pork mixed together
1 egg
1/2 cup Italian bread crumbs
1/4 cup milk
1 small onion, chopped
fresh parsley, chopped
1 teaspoon garlic powder
1 teaspoon basil or fresh basil
Pinch salt and pepper

In large bowl, mix ground chuck or ground turkey and ground pork. Add all other ingredients and form meatballs no larger than two inches but not too small. These are not the other kind of meatballs. Place in pan. Put under broiler to lightly brown both sides. No need to cook all the way through, as they are going right into the sauce.

Mama Rose's Tomato Sauce

3–4 cloves fresh garlic, minced
extra-virgin olive oil
basil
oregano
salt
pepper
12 fresh tomatoes out of garden, if you have them, or 2 large cans Italian canned plum tomatoes, whole or crushed (or 1 of each)
1 can tomato paste, if fresh tomatoes
2 tablespoons sugar
red wine

Heat oil in large saucepan on medium. Add garlic just to soften. Squish the whole tomatoes or cut up and add to pot. Add entire can of tomato paste. Add one can of water of large sauce can. Mix all herbs and sugar into sauce. Let simmer on medium to low heat for at least 40 minutes. Add splash of vino *rosso*. Fresh basil is worth it, if you have it, also on top of pasta with the cheese. Enjoy over homemade or regular pasta. If desired, try spinach, artichoke, or whole-wheat pasta. The best!

Quick and Fresh Pasta Pomodoro Sauce

This is my favorite sauce. There are many tomato pasta sauces. This one makes a great summer dish. It goes well with steaks on the grill or drunken chicken.

6-8 fresh tomatoes preferably (or 2 large cans, if unavailable), cut in bite-size pieces
3 cloves fresh garlic, minced
2 cups fresh basil, broken up
Dash salt and pepper
½ 1 cup extra-virgin olive oil

Mix all ingredients. Mash it up a little so the juices all blend together. If you desire, do a quick sauté or microwave sauce for 2 minutes to heat up.

Boil about a pound of vermicelli or angel hair and cover it with the sauce. Sprinkle Parmigiano/Romano cheese on top. New York strip steak can only be used as an accompaniment (just kidding).

Drunken Chicken

2 whole chickens
rub (oregano, parsley, garlic powder, salt, pepper, thyme, rosemary)
2 tablespoons olive oil
2 cans of favorite beer

This is usually a grill experience, but it can go in the oven too. After washing chickens, coat with olive oil and rub with spices. Stand the whole chickens on top of open beer cans and place on grill. Bake for at least 2 hours at 350 degrees F or under grill cover. No need to turn or disturb. Eat this with the fresh tomato garlic pasta and you have one of the famous Martino Sunday feasts. Just add some garlic bread or fresh Italian bread. Delizioso.

Cod or Shrimp Stir-Fry

olive oil
4 cloves garlic, minced
1 onion, sliced
2 sweet peppers, sliced
2 pieces of cod or another white fish, fresh or frozen
1 dozen medium-large raw shrimp, deveined and tail on or off
Pinch curry
Pinch turmeric
Handful of Italian parsley chopped
Splash of white wine Worcestershire sauce
3–4 cups spinach and baby kale
2 tablespoons red chili sauce
quinoa, wild rice, brown rice, or farro

In large saucepan, heat oil and add garlic, onion, and peppers until softened. Add fish, spices, and Worcestershire sauce. Top with greens and cover. Cook until fish looks cooked, about 10 minutes. Add red chili sauce, mix everything together, and remove from heat. Cook grains separately. Let sit until grains are done. Cover grain with mixture for a delicious, exotic, and healthy quick meal.

Baked Salmon

4 ounce piece of Alaskan wild salmon, fresh or frozen
Splash of white wine Worcestershire sauce
Sprinkle parsley
Dash black or white pepper
spray olive oil or drizzle
1 teaspoon lemon juice

In baking pan, place salmon. Add all other ingredients to salmon. Bake at 350 degrees F for 20–25 minutes until cooked through but still moist.

Serve with a sweet potato with cinnamon and pepper, and a kale salad. How healthy is this meal?

Swiss Chard, White Bean, and Sausage Stew

1 pound Swiss chard, any color
1 pound Italian sausage or sweet turkey sausage, sliced into 1/2-inch chunks
1 onion, chopped
3 cloves garlic, minced
paprika
cayenne
turmeric
2 cups drained and rinsed white beans, cannellini, or navy beans
3 cups canned low-sodium chicken broth or vegetable broth
1 cup water
Italian bread
shredded Italian cheese
olive oil

In medium pot with water, add chard and cook for 3 minutes. Drain and set aside. In large pot, heat oil over medium heat. Add sausage, onions, garlic, and spices until meat is brown, about 5 minutes. Add water, chard, beans, and broth. Bring to simmer about 15 minutes. Sprinkle with shredded Parmigiano or Romano. Serve with a rustic, full-bodied vino. Have some fresh Italian pane to soak up the goodness. This is one comfort meal on a cold night.

Roasted Cornish Game Hen

1 hen
1 medium onion, chopped
2 cloves garlic, minced
3–4 carrots washed, cut in horizontal 1-inch pieces
4 large mushrooms, cleaned and sliced
olive oil spray
dash cinnamon
1 teaspoon brown sugar
herbs de Provence (or rosemary, thyme, parsley, turmeric, sage, pepper, salt)

Place rinsed Cornish hen in middle of roasting pan. Place some onion and garlic inside cavity. Add all other ingredients to pan. Spray hen with olive oil and season with spices. Spray vegetables, and sprinkle a little cinnamon and brown sugar over carrots. Cover and bake at 350 degrees for about 30 minutes. A great side for this dish is wild rice or quinoa mix.

Soft Tacos

6 small flour tortillas
1 pound steak strips or pork, similar to fajita size, thin
1 medium onion, sliced thinly
4 cloves garlic, minced
1–2 large/medium zucchini peeled, sliced into 1/4-inch discs
2–3 tablespoons vegetable or coconut oil (any oil with high smoke point)
1 cup tomatillo sauce or favorite taco sauce

2 tablespoons adobe spice blend (including paprika, cumin, chili pepper, black pepper, salt)

1/2 cup sour cream

1 cup thinly shredded cheddar or mixed cheeses

1 avocado, peeled and mashed

In large saucepan, in heated oil on medium, lightly brown zucchini discs. Set aside. In same pan, sauté beef/pork strips with onion and garlic. Add spice blend to coat all meat. You may not need to add any additional oil if cooked quickly. Warm tortillas. Build the taco with layering of: choice of sauce, zucchini, cheese, steak/pork/onion, and top with a dollop of sour cream and or avocado. Roll up and enjoy. (These tacos are delish with fish, too. I use cod. Substitute the sour cream and taco sauce with a creamy garlic dressing, with mayonnaise and buttermilk, parsley, mustard, and garlic.)

Pizza

pizza dough, any kind, any size, round (ingredient amounts depend on size of pizza—you decide)

sliced tomatoes

sweet pepper, chopped

red onion or sweet onion, chopped

broccoli, cut small pieces

cooked chicken, chopped

spinach, chopped

dash salt, pepper and garlic

Parmigiano cheese

mozzarella cheese

olive oil

Making a pizza should be creative. I start with a sauce of tomato or pesto. Then I layer cut-up vegetables and chicken, or just vegetables. I drizzle olive oil, add spices, and sprinkle Parmigiano cheese. I top it with mozzarella and/or ricotta. Bake 13–15 minutes until melted and lightly browned, on middle rack of oven at 350–400 degrees F. Just watch it; do not burn. Easy and homemade.

Sweet Red Relish Shrimp Stir-Fry

12 large shrimp, tails off and deveined
1 medium onion, chopped
2 cloves garlic, minced
2 tablespoons peanut or sesame oil
3 tablespoons sweet red pepper relish
½ teaspoon ginger
1/2 teaspoon soy sauce
1/2 teaspoon basil
1–2 cups broccoli slaw
1 cup snow peas or can of regular green peas
1–2 cups arugula
optional: 2 cups brown rice, wild rice, Jasmine rice, couscous, or quinoa

In skillet, sauté onion and garlic until softened. Add shrimp, cooking until pink. Top with arugula, slaw, peas, spices, and relish. Mix all over low heat until softened and all flavors are savory. Serve over choice of grains if desired.

Spicy Asian White Fish Stir-Fry

1 pound or 4 pieces cod fish
1 large onion, chopped
4 garlic cloves, minced
6 ounces mixed mushrooms (oyster, shitake, enoki, morels, etc.)
1–2 cups broccoli slaw
1–2 cups kale cut in small pieces, stems removed
1 bunch asparagus, ends removed and cut into 1-inch pieces
curry
ginger
turmeric
1/2 teaspoon soy sauce
1–2 tablespoons red chili sauce
3 tablespoons coconut or sesame or peanut oil
optional: Jasmine rice, sticky rice, brown rice

In large saucepan, heat oil. Add fish, onion, and garlic and asparagus. Add mushrooms for last 2 minutes. Cook until tender and fish is browned. Add kale, slaw, and spices. Mix well until blended and deliciously aromatic. Serve over rice, if desired.

Contorno—Side Dishes / Vegetables

Kale Salad

1 large bag or 2–3 bunches of kale
lemon juice of 2 lemons
1/2–1 cup grated Parmigiano cheese
1/2 cup extra-virgin olive oil
2 tablespoons red pepper flakes, optional
rice vinegar, champagne vinegar, or white wine vinegar to taste
salt to taste
garlic powder to taste

Wash kale. Strip thick stems and dispose of them. Cut up leaves. In large bowl, combine kale, oil, lemon juice, vinegar, and spices. Mix well. When ready to serve, add Parmigiano cheese. Serve as side to just about anything.

Caprese Salad

1–2 large beefsteak tomato (yellow or red), cut in 1/4-inch slices
1 pound fresh mozzarella cheese, sliced
1/2 cup fresh basil
Dash salt and pepper
drizzle extra-virgin olive oil over tomatoes and cheese
drizzle balsamic vinegar at end tomatoes and cheese

On salad plate, alternate slices of tomato and cheese pieces in circle. Drizzle olive oil and vinegar over all. Add salt, pepper, and torn basil as topping. This salad is best with fresh mozzarella.

Broccoli Rabe and Garlic

2 tablespoons olive oil
2 cloves garlic, minced
16 ounces broccoli rabe, rinsed, trimmed, and cut into 1-inch pieces
lemon juice to taste
dash salt and pepper

Heat oil and garlic in large nonstick skillet over medium heat until garlic softens. Add greens and little water to simmer. Cover, reduce to simmer for about 8–10 minutes until tender. Drain. Drizzle olive oil and lemon juice, and sprinkle salt and pepper. This could be served as a side or as a base for a protein, such as fish. Very healthy and pretty.

Cucumber Salad

4 small cucumbers, halved and cut lengthwise into 1/4-inch slices
1 small red onion, thinly sliced
1/4 cup fresh fennel, cut into small pieces
1/4 cup rice vinegar and olive oil combined
3 tablespoons fresh dill chopped
Dash salt and pepper

Toss cucumbers, fennel, and onions in bowl. Set aside. Mix oil, vinegar, dill, salt, and pepper until smooth. Toss over vegetable mixture.

Beet Blue Cheese Salad

1 can red beets, quartered
1/2 cup chopped red cabbage
1/4 cup chopped red onion
2 tablespoons crumbled blue cheese
1 tablespoon chopped walnuts
1/4 cup balsamic vinegar and extra-virgin olive oil
Dash salt and pepper

I use canned red beets. It's easier and just as tasty. Fresh beets take quite a long time to cook. If you have the time, they will be great. Drain can of beets. Place in bowl with cabbage and onion. Mix with oil and vinegar and spices. Top with blue cheese and walnuts.

Zucchini Boats

2 large zucchini squash, halved lengthwise, ends trimmed
1 egg
1 cup Italian bread crumbs
2 cloves garlic, minced
3 tablespoons olive oil
1/2 cup grated Parmigiano or Romano cheese
Dash salt and pepper
1 teaspoon basil
1/8 teaspoon oregano
2 tablespoons parsley

Scoop out center of squash with teaspoon, careful not to tear boat. Cut up in small pieces. In large bowl, add squash and all other ingredients. Mix well. Spray baking pan with olive oil and heat oven to 375 degrees F. Stuff zucchini boats with filling. Lightly spray top of each boat with olive oil or drizzle and place in pan. Bake uncovered for 30–35 minutes until lightly brown and squash is soft but firm to touch. If desired, drizzle olive oil and additional cheese over boats upon serving.

Swiss Chard with Fresh Pomodoro and Garlic

2 heads rainbow, red, or white Swiss chard, trimmed ends and washed thoroughly
3 cloves garlic, minced
1 small onion, chopped
2 tablespoons olive oil
6 plum tomatoes, quartered
Dash salt and pepper

In large skillet or saucepan, lightly mix oil, garlic, onion, and tomatoes, about 3 minutes. Add cut-up chard and mix until softened and all flavors blended. If desired, this could be a delicious main dish over a bed of pasta with lots of shaved or grated Romano or Parmigiano cheese. No need for a sauce; this would be enough to mix over pasta with a drizzle of olive oil.

Spaghetti Squash

1 small or medium-size spaghetti squash
Choice of either pesto sauce, tomato sauce, butter, or olive oil, to taste
Sprinkle on grated Parmigiano cheese

In large pot, fill water to cover squash. Boil on low or medium until able to pierce squash with fork. Remove squash and slice in half. Remove and discard seeds. Using fork, pull out "spaghetti" part of squash with a scraping motion. Place all squash in dish and add your favorite toppings. This is a main dish or side, depending on taste.

Cauliflower Fritters

1 head cauliflower
1/4 cup Italian bread crumbs
2 eggs
1 cup mixed cheddar and mozzarella
1/4 cup chopped scallions
3 tablespoons olive oil
dash of red pepper
sour cream

Cut up cauliflower in pieces and cook until tender. In bowl, mash up all pieces and then add eggs, cheese, scallions, and bread crumbs. Make small patties. Cook until browned on both sides. Serve with side of sour cream.

Mediterranean Flavor Salad

1–2 cups mixed baby greens (lettuce/spinach/basil/arugula/dandelion)
2–4 artichoke hearts, halved
equal amounts peas and julienned carrots
2–4 Sicilian olives or big black Greek olives

Asiago cheese, grated or shredded
fresh parsley

Mix all ingredients with orange-cranberry vinaigrette dressing for an excellent accompaniment to a seafood main course.

Orange-Cranberry Vinaigrette

8 ounces orange juice
4 ounces cranberry juice
4 ounces olive oil
Dash kosher or sea salt and pepper
3 tablespoons each of chopped herbs (basil, parsley, and mint)
orange zest to garnish

Blend all ingredients in processor or blender. Excellent choice to serve with seafood as main course.

Mustard Vinaigrette

1 tablespoon dark mustard
1/4 cup white or red wine vinegar
1/2 cup olive oil
1/8 teaspoon of dill, thyme, and parsley
Whisk together ingredients in bowl.

Uncle Sam's French Dressing

1 can tomato soup
3/4 cup sugar
2/3 cup oil, vegetable or olive
2/3 cup cider vinegar
1 teaspoon salt

Put all ingredients in blender for one minute or whisk together. Pour over favorite salad.

Celery Salad

3 cups chopped celery, ends trimmed
2 tablespoons shallots, cut up

Dressing:
1/4 cup lemon juice
1/2 cup olive oil
2 teaspoons lemon zest
1/8 teaspoon salt and pepper
1 teaspoon celery seeds
1/2 teaspoon anchovy paste
Top with shaved Parmigiano cheese
1 tablespoon of walnuts, chopped

Place celery and shallots in bowl. In small bowl, mix all other ingredients. Pour over celery and top with cheese and walnuts.

Citrus Dressing

2 cups olive oil
1 cup sugar
juice of 2 limes
1 1/2 cups cilantro
2 cloves garlic
salt
pepper

Blend all ingredients in processor or blender. Delicious over salads as well as seafood.

Creamy Garlic Dressing

½ cup mayonnaise or Miracle Whip
1 cup buttermilk
¼ cup chopped parsley
2 tablespoons mustard of choice

3 cloves garlic, minced

Blend all ingredients in processor or blender.

Dolce—Desserts

Mom's Apple Pie

Double-crust pie (10-inch plate):

2 cups all-purpose flour

1 teaspoon salt

3/4 cup well-chilled all-vegetable shortening

4–8 tablespoons ice-cold water

Filling:

8 medium-size apples (3 granny smith, 3 golden delicious, and 2 Macintosh or Cortland varieties)

3/4 cup sugar

1/2 teaspoon cinnamon

1/2 teaspoon nutmeg

In large bowl, prepare filling with peeled, cored, thinly sliced apples. Add sugar, cinnamon, and nutmeg and toss. Set aside.

In large bowl, blend flour and salt. Cut shortening into flour mixture with pastry blender or fork. Stir in just enough water with fork until dough holds together. Divide dough into two balls. Roll out one, a little larger, for bottom crust on lightly floured surface, about 2 inches wider than pie plate. Place in plate and trim edges even with plate. Fill unbaked crust with apple mixture. Roll out remaining crust for top of pie. Place on top, trim edges, flute edges together to seal pie. Cut slits in top crust or prick with fork to vent steam. Brush top crust with milk and sprinkle with sugar.

Preheat oven to 375 degrees. Cook for 20 minutes. Reduce heat to 350 degrees, and cook for another 45 minutes until browned and juices begin to bubble through slits in crust.

Mom's Apple Strudel

*Dough is same for double-crust apple pie.

Filling:
2 apples, one granny smith and one golden delicious (or your choices)
1 tablespoon flour
1/2 teaspoon cinnamon
4 tablespoons sugar
1/4 cup raisins, white or brown
1/3 cup maraschino cherries, chopped
1/4 cup coconut flakes
1/4 cup walnuts, chopped

Roll out large circle of dough, about 16 inches. Spread apple mixture over crust evenly. Roll up, similar to jelly roll, pressing firmly as you roll and tuck in ends of strudel. Make about six small slits on top of roll. Wash with cherry juice and sprinkle with sugar.

Grease baking sheet or baking pan lightly. Bake for 1 hour in preheated 350 degrees F until golden brown and juices are bubbly. When removed from oven, while still warm, cut into 2-inch slices and sprinkle with powdered sugar. (This is definitely one of my most favorite desserts in the world!)

Mom's Peach Pie

*Prepare dough same as for double-crust apple pie. The top crust will be made into a lattice design by cutting even strips to cover the peach mixture. Preheat oven to 350 degrees F and bake for 1 hour until brown and juices are bubbly.

Filling:
10 large ripe peaches, peeled and thinly sliced
3/4 cup sugar
1/2 cup tapioca

Mix in bowl and add to unbaked pie crust. First dough is bottom of pie. Roll out second dough and cut into about ten strips to create a lattice effect. Flute edges and sprinkle sugar on top.

Martino Family Christmas Fig Cookies

Cookie dough:

2 pounds all-purpose flour

4 eggs

3/4 cup cold water

Mix all ingredients on counter or marble slab. Make thin rolls of dough and cut off 1 inch for each cookie. Roll out into 4–5-inch circles. Use flour to keep dough strong, not too thin, as it will be manipulated and formed to make the many designs of these tasty unique gems.

Cookie filling:

3 pounds dried figs

1 pound pitted dates

1 orange peel

1 jar of maraschino cherries, drained

1/2 pound walnuts

8-ounce jar honey

Much love

On lightly greased cookie sheets, place cookies about 2 inches apart. At 350 degrees F, bake for 10–15 minutes, until light brown. Do not overcook. When cooled, sprinkle lightly with confectioner's sugar.

We had a most unique machine that my father used to grind up all these tasty ingredients to make the filling for our Christmas cookies. It was an old-fashioned meat grinder with the handle to turn. It churned out just the right consistency for our little cookies. One teaspoon of this filling was enough. If it was too much, you would know immediately, and the dough would not work well. My father made the fanciest ones. Everyone who ever received these as a gift loved to see and eat the little "chickens" he would mold out of dough. We all tried to make those but were always encouraged to make our own and be creative. As with many things, Dad had the touch that was impossible to duplicate. There were Christmas wreaths, snowmen, angels, and many other favorites. This was a planned event in our house. A few times, a visiting friend would be informed we were making the cookies that night, and they were invited to stay and participate. The family would sit around the dining or kitchen table for hours on end talking, laughing, and sipping brandy until all the dough and filling was gone.

As my mother rolled out each little circle for us, she would attend the oven and cook them to perfection. We would make dozens! At the end of the evening, we had our own cookie tasting and enjoyed the fruits of our labor. This was a yearly tradition right before Christmas. There were many Christmas tins of these gems offered as gifts throughout the season. The time spent together around that table for one night, no matter how many hours it took, was one of my happiest holiday memories. Definitely, one of our delightful Christmas traditions was "making the cookies." To this day, friends and family still talk about the Martino's fig cookies, and now they will have the recipe. I know they will add their love.

Brown Betty Apple Crisp

4–6 apples peeled and sliced
1–2 cups Bisquick
1/2 cup uncooked whole oatmeal
Dash of cinnamon and nutmeg
Dash of apple pie spice
1/4 cup walnuts
1/4 cup milk or coconut milk or water
1/3 cup butter or olive oil spread

Heat oven to 375 degrees F. In glass or nonstick 9 x 9 lightly greased pan, layer apples. Mix dry ingredients in bowl with spices and nuts and milk. Add in butter. Drop over apples evenly. Bake 30 minutes. Remove, cover, and let rest. Serve with vanilla ice cream or frozen yogurt over warm crisp.

Peach Crisp

6 cups sliced peaches
2 tablespoons honey
2 tablespoons cornstarch
1 cup flour
1/3 cup brown sugar
1/4 cup old-fashioned oats
4 tablespoons margarine or butter
3 tablespoons pecans, chopped

In bowl, toss peaches, honey, and cornstarch. Set aside. Combine flour, sugar, oats, and margarine. Add pecans and toss lightly. In medium baking dish, place peaches. Sprinkle oat mixture on top. Bake at 350 degrees F for 45 minutes or golden. Allow to cool before serving. Top with some frozen yogurt or favorite ice cream, if desired.

Apple Treat for One

1 large red delicious apple, seeded and sliced, peeled if desired
1 teaspoon lemon juice
1/4 cup caramel sauce
1 tablespoon walnuts
whipped cream, real stuff

In a small bowl, toss apple with lemon juice. Cover with caramel and nuts. Toss until coated. Top with whipped cream of choice. Add a cup of hot, freshly brewed coffee, cappuccino, or tea. If you have a fireplace, it is a good place to curl up on the couch with this treat.

Pumpkin Cannoli

1 (15-ounce) can 100 percent pumpkin, no sugar added
15 ounces ricotta cheese
2 teaspoons pumpkin pie spice
3 packets stevia
confectioner's sugar to sprinkle on finished gems

3 tablespoons chopped or crushed pistachios to dip in ends, if desired
1 box mini cannoli shells

In large bowl, mix together the pumpkin, ricotta, stevia, and spice until creamy. Using piping or plastic bag with end cut, fill the cannoli shells. Dip one end in crushed pistachios. Sprinkle with powdered sugar. Remember, my advice is always to take the cannolis.

Zucchini Bread

This is not usually a dessert but is best served as a side for a vegetarian dish or, of course, pasta.
3 cups diced zucchini (do not peel)
1 medium onion, finely chopped
1 cup Bisquick
4 eggs
1/2 cup olive oil
1/2 cup grated Parmigiano cheese
Dash of salt and pepper

Mix all ingredients in bowl and place in greased baking dish or loaf pan. Bake for 45–60 minutes at 350 degrees F.

Succo—Juices/Smoothies

My Favorite Homemade Juice

4 apples
8 carrots
1 bunch fresh parsley

8 stalks celery
1 cucumber

You need a juicer. I cut up everything just small enough to fit through the tube. No peeling. Wash and remove any thick stems. Most delicious, refreshing, full of vitamins, fresh juice ever. Save the pulp for a soup, and you have literally just eaten the whole thing. You can make this every day, and your body will love it.

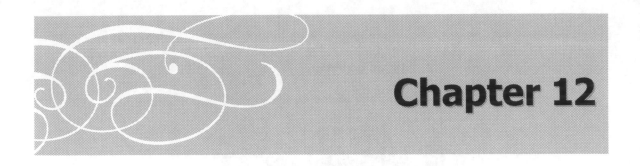

Chapter 12

Water, Wine, Coffee, Tea

Nothing is softer or more flexible than water, yet nothing can resist it.
—Lao Tzu

Aqua, Vino, Café, Te—Water, Wine, Coffee, Tea
Water

Water is the elixir of life. We were fortunate to have an artesian well on the farm, something many people have never even seen. I remember going into the well house and drinking from the continuous flow of ice-cold, bubbling, pure delicious water. New York state is definitely known for its amazing water. I suggest that if you want to not shrivel up like an old prune, drink at least thirty-two ounces a day. Just a thought about bottled water: you probably do not need it to survive. I prefer filling a container from the tap or filter system and keeping it cold in the refrigerator. However, if you are in Fiji, little bottles of Fiji water are everywhere. I do believe that is one of the best artesian spring waters on the planet.

There are so many choices of water on the shelves these days. I wonder just how many ways you can "make" water. Coconut water is a staple in my refrigerator. I love it ice cold, and I water it down with water. It can be very sweet, and I love water, so I lower the sugar. Electrolytes abound in this life-saving elixir. If ever on a desert island and there are coconut palms, you may survive. Of note, coconut water or coconut milk can be a natural laxative. It is a great source of protein too.

Most refreshing is the *frizzante*. Sparkling water, seltzer, mineral water, Italian sparkling water all come to mind. These are refreshing, invigorating, and good for you. If you desire, add a twist of lemon, lime, cucumber, orange, mint, or just lots of cubes. As offered in the many spas I have visited, cucumber water can help eliminate the toxins after a day of pampering. Also, seltzer is a great accompaniment with any meal, as well as after dinner to settle the stomach.

Another sweet memory of my travels is of Massimiliano, a true descendent of the gladiators, serving the aqua frizzante around the stone grotto pool fed by the Mediterranean Sea. A wonderful memory of my visit to the little town of San Remo on the Italian Riviera. Bellinis enjoyed on the Royal Hotel stone *terrazza* nightly, bring beautiful sunsets to mind. This was a wonderful time in a magical place.

Mineral water is probably the best to drink. Unfortunately, the carbonated choices may contain phosphorus and therefore inhibit calcium absorption, if overdone. This is also a problem with too much caffeine.

Water is the most neutral on the pH scale. To function in the best balance is around 7.4. Water is a 7 on the scale. Pure acid is 0. Too much acidity in the body can lead to dysfunction in many areas. Dis-ease is the result. That is another reason I feel better when I am eating mainly fruits and vegetables. Eating an anti-inflammatory diet and keeping your liver and lungs healthy is helpful in maintaining a more neutral state. Remember, once again, moderation and balance is the best way.

I personally cannot identify with many bottled soda drinks. We had Coca-Cola and ginger ale in our house, usually as a medicinal item. It was not served regularly on a daily basis. It was good for an upset stomach or if we were just not feeling well. So you see, there are other reasons to drink some of these sugary drinks. I have seen an unbelievable addiction to these drinks in society, which I believe adds to many diseases and other health problems. The diet ones are not a good alternative either. Check your sodium and caffeine intake on those. They are in the high-acidic range of your pH scale.

> *Wine is bottled poetry.*
> —Robert Lewis Stevenson

Wine

Vino, vino, vino. Che bella vino! Vino rosso, bianco, spumante, cava, prosecco—so many grapes, so little time. Wine has always been a staple in my home. Cooking, drinking, and gifting. Wine can always be a great gift to bring when visiting. As my father, Joe, would say, "You do not go to someone's home empty-handed." He would always have a bag of fresh picked red delicious apples out of our orchards, one of my mother, Rose's, famous apple pies or strudel, or a bottle of red wine when we ventured to a friend or family's home. To this day, I try to carry that tradition whenever I plan a visit.

The most common red grapes in Italy are the Sangiovese wines. The most famous red wines are from the Tuscany region of Florence and Siena, and the Chianti region. Valpolicella has a lighter flavor. Marsala, a sweeter wine, was always in our house. We would have a little sip to make us strong. My grandmother, Lena, would suggest a raw egg in some marsala to give us strong blood. We did not always agree on that!

In my travels to Australia, I enjoyed the shiraz varieties of red wines. I still like to keep an extra bottle in the wine rack. I can remember an evening when visiting Australia. I stayed on Darling Harbor in Sydney. One dinner comes to mind. I tried barramundi, a delicious Asian sea bass, and free-range angus beef. The wonderful food Down Under was a culinary journey. The only thing I did not care for was the Vegemite, a vegetable paste. If my memory serves me correctly, it was extremely salty, allegedly comparable to peanut butter, as it is high in protein.

Pairing wines with food is an art. The traditional white wine with fish and red with beef no longer serves our more educated palates and experience with the grapes. We have a wine for every course of our meals, as well as every special event. When entertaining, I try to incorporate the appetizer as well as the dessert wines into my menu. It makes the dinner party more festive, and my guests always remember the courses and how delicious they were with the additional vino accompaniment. Champagne and bubbly prosecco are always received well at a celebratory event, and fresh strawberries in the glass add to the fun.

I do believe red wine is actually good for you, but so is grape juice. It is the resveratrol that gives you the healthy reason for imbibing. I do not really need a reason. I believe red wine can and should be paired with almost any meal in *The Farmer's Daughter's Guide*. Many people choose to enjoy a glass daily. You might enjoy a savory bread with cheese, oil, garlic, or plain Italian bread as an accompaniment. Growing up, I can remember a rather large bottle of chianti always on the table, or on the floor by the table, at every meal and every card game. My grandfather, Ignazio, would have the smallest glass in the house on hand and would allow us to have just a little taste of the vino. Just a reminder on alcohol: moderation is the best.

I cook with wine every chance I can. No wine goes to waste in my house. If a bottle is open, it will be used. I love to add red wine to sauté mushrooms and onions. White wine in some stir-fry dishes can be great with fish. I have been known to splash a little vino *rosso* in the spaghetti sauce too. It is great as a reduction for a ragu sauce with vegetables over pasta any day.

Coffee

There has been overwhelming advice over the years about the enjoyment of coffee. I have never stopped drinking it and never will. I love the flavor of coffee, and I do not drink decaf. I have at least two wonderful caffeine-laden cups with Italian creamer in the morning before I start my day. I do not use sugar, because the sugar-free Italian creamer is the best flavor, no sweetener needed. I love espresso with a little lemon rind across the rim, maybe a teaspoon of sugar, if I am in the mood. Of note, if you are a regular coffee drinker, you may notice a slight headache if you have not had your usual dose of caffeine. Caffeine withdrawal can cause headaches, so if you wish to eliminate it from your diet, this may be a side effect.

Cappuccino is always a festive brew when out to dinner, or if you have the wonderful machine to steam your milk, then enjoy it. I love coffee ice cream, cakes, anything at all with the flavor of those beans. I even love dark-chocolate-covered coffee beans. Kahlua liqueur is a warm welcome on a cold evening. With coffee establishments on every corner and shopping center, it is safe to say coffee is good. Obviously, my only concern is the caffeine content, so if you are drinking coffee, try to limit your cups and the sugar. Too many spikes in your blood sugar are never healthy.

Tea

Every week, I make a large pitcher of green tea and keep it in the refrigerator. You can add lemon and a little sugar if you must, but I prefer it virgin and green. Once in a while, I will add a bag of bergamot or citrus-flavored black tea to mix it up. The health and medicinal reasons to enjoy tea outnumber any other beverage except water, of course, so drink it. At least two cups or glasses a day is worth the effort. I prefer to make it homemade, as the prepared items today tend to include too much sugar. Teas with added fresh fruit can be a delight. I sometimes will freeze berries in ice cubes and use those for my iced tea or seltzer. The choices are endless, and so are the benefits. Green tea has phenols, an antioxidant and cancer fighter. The Japanese drink a lot of this, and their cancer rate is much lower than many countries. I think it is also good for your skin, as it is very hydrating.

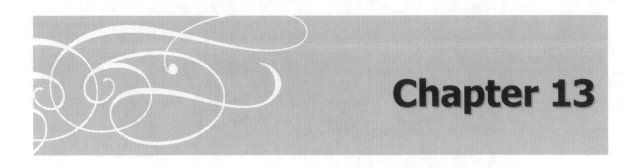

Chapter 13

Vitamins, Antioxidants, and Supplements

Let food be thy medicine and medicine be thy food.
—Hippocrates

I am a firm believer in supplements. When you analyze nutritional benefits of most foods, you find that it almost is impossible to ingest the amount of food to accommodate what your body needs in the vitamin content. My biggest concern in nutrition is having a solid base of antioxidants in your body. I not only eat with this in mind, but I make sure I take a balanced regimen of them. They fight for you, literally. They keep your heart, brain, and immune system healthy, as well as slowing the aging process. I can honestly boast that I never get sick. Meaning, if there is a cold or bug around me, I do not catch the germ. If I do, my body will fight it. I am so fortunate to have a healthy immune system. That is my mantra to any clients. I always say, keep your immune system healthy, and you will be able to fight off most any bug or disease. Our body is a wondrous machine and knows how to keep things homeostatic, if we let it. There are free radicals out of our control, but we can do our best to stay healthy preventatively, not just when we feel a symptom.

I can never understand when someone says, "I do not feel well, so I am packing myself full of Echinacea and vitamin C." My usual response is, "Why not take the C on a regular basis, not just when not feeling well. By then, your body is already in the fight mode and needs rest and fuel to be able to do the job of healing." Most people, once again, do not allow their body to rest when they feel sick. Have you ever noticed how people go to work sick? They feel they need to save sick time for vacation. The well people they work with may have a different opinion.

A list of my favorite antioxidants and supplements for a daily routine include: alpha lipoic acid, vitamin E, Co-Q10, vitamin C, folic acid, biotin, and vitamin B6. Selenium and Ginkgo biloba are also important. Some of these are fat-soluble, and others water-soluble. Ginkgo and E are blood thinners so need to be considered if you are on a medication for this.

The pomegranate is a powerhouse of antioxidants, fighting heart disease, cancer, and aging. It is an interesting fruit that takes a little effort to eat but is very tasty. Pomegranate juice is so refreshing when paired with seltzer and a squirt or two of lime juice over ice. It's a nice substitute for ice tea or lemonade on a hot, sticky day. I find it to be a good diuretic as well.

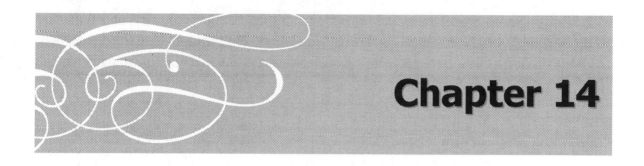

Chapter 14

Superfoods

Life itself is the proper binge.
—Julia Child

There are many superfoods in my opinion. Unfortunately, many people shy away from some of them without full knowledge of what they are missing in taste or nutrition. I am particularly fond of greens. I will eat just about anything that is green. I spent a big part of my life watching horses graze on the emerald clover pastures of our farm. They had their daily grains too and homegrown hay. My father's special blend of barley or wheat, mixed with of molasses and carob, kept them healthy and strong. This was a mixture he fed to our thoroughbred racehorses as well. As special treats, they had all the apples and carrots they could eat. Our dogs had vegetables in their bowls too. Everyone ate well on the farm!

Many people have begun to realize the importance of spirulina and add that to their smoothies. But I prefer the real vegetable out of the garden, such as spinach, kale, Swiss chard, escarole, collard and mustard greens, beet and turnip greens, cabbage, and bok choy. I love all of them. Cook them in any dish, as a side, or in soups. Remember, if you boil them, save the water and drink it. I chill it for a vitamin detox. They are sure to keep you well supplied with iron, vitamins C, D, and A, magnesium, and lots of fiber. In preparing a meal, remember the more colors, the healthier it is.

I believe in eating and using as much from the sea as I can. I love all kinds of seafood and eat it weekly. I have become very fond of seaweed, kelp or algae, and try to incorporate that in my meals, soups, and appetizers. I love to add a little red pepper, rice vinegar, and sesame seeds to the seaweed you can order at any sushi bar. Seaweed and algae are rich in minerals and omega-3s and have an alkalizing effect on the acidity of our body. Iodine is a very beneficial mineral found in seaweed. The thyroid gland benefits from iodine. Remember the fifth taste, umami? Many skincare products today are enriched with sea minerals or plants.

Dairy is very important. Unfortunately, lactose intolerance is quite common. There are many ways to still incorporate dairy into your diet, and the variations of milk are mentioned in the pyramid. I love dairy products and eat them daily. Cheese can go on anything in my kitchen. Greek yogurt is the kind I prefer. The stronger the cheese, the better for you, so blue cheese on salads is a great addition.

Eggs are a complete little meal. One hard-boiled egg can be a perfect quick meal with a little salt and pepper, and it's loaded with protein. Egg whites are a great substitution or addition to any egg dish, but I always like to add a whole egg for all the nutrition. Do not fear the cholesterol question that many have about eating too many eggs. In fact, the egg yolk is the most concentrated source of choline, which actually assists in cell structure and lipid (fat) transport. Eggs also have lutein to promote good eye health. Eggs are so easy to cook, and if you can get fresh eggs from a farm, or raise one or two chickens of your own, you are very lucky. We had a farmer who sold the best brown eggs in our town. They were guaranteed the freshest. If you have the opportunity to buy fresh eggs from a farmer, I suggest you do so. Yes, you can taste the difference!

Animal protein does have a nutritional value. Of course, many people prefer the vegetarian diet, but if you can incorporate salmon or turkey breast in your diet, you will be satisfied with the result. Try a Greek yogurt sauce, and you have a tasty and healthy entrée. Omega-3s are a necessary nutrient as well as micronutrients that your body needs. Some vegetarians require a B vitamin supplement if they do not have enough protein in their diet.

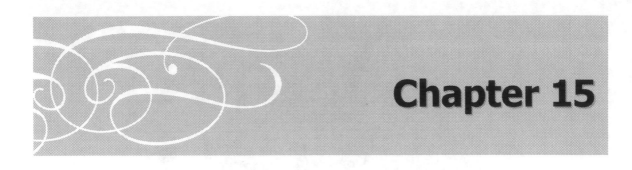

Chapter 15

Just for Fun

My weaknesses have always been food and men—in that order.
—Dolly Parton

Eating healthy is a great start, and for most, that may be all that matters. Personally, I believe it cannot hurt to look good too. I have been blessed with the true Italian look of dark hair, big dark eyes, and olive skin. That is not a bad combination, but like everything else, it needs to be pampered and taken care of. I love to mix up some kitchen remedies for the face, neck, and décolletage and make believe I went to the spa, which is easier on the budget too. These are foods that are easily accessible and probably in your refrigerator as you read this, so get mixing. Put on some music and take a few minutes to chill out.

Vinegar
Skin toners can be expensive, drying, and sometimes just useless. This is an old remedy, and of course apple cider vinegar has to be the most basic kind. I have a bottle in the refrigerator at all times. After washing your face, mix one tablespoon with two cups of water. This will tighten up any sad facial skin. I also use witch hazel as a great toner.

Milk
Milk facials are so rejuvenating. Make a quick paste mask with a quarter cup of powdered milk and water. Coat your face with the mixture and let it dry completely. Rinse with warm water. Hello, fresh face.

Banana

Banana equals Botox. Bananas are good for moisturizing and firming. Mash up medium banana to paste. Apply to your face for about ten minutes. Rinse with cold water. I feel good just writing this.

Yogurt

Plain yogurt may not be so tasty, but your skin likes it. Mix up a quarter cup of yogurt, two tablespoons honey, and a medium banana. Actually, this could be breakfast too. Let set for about fifteen minutes and rinse off. For tighter pores, just the yogurt. You have a yummy face. Do not forget the fragile décolletage if you ever plan on showing some cleavage.

Oatmeal

Oatmeal soap can be a great body exfoliator in the shower. But for a quick facial, try a half cup hot, *not* boiling, water and one-third cup oatmeal. Mix it up. Add two tablespoons of plain yogurt, some honey, and one small egg white. Apply a thin layer of this to your face, relax for about ten to fifteen minutes, and rinse with warm water. One word of advice: do not let the oats clog the drain.

Mayonnaise

I would rather spread this over my face instead of food, so if you have some whole-egg mayonnaise in the refrigerator, spread some over your face and leave on for twenty minutes. Wipe it off and rinse with cool water. It leaves a soft and smooth face.

Baking Soda and Coconut Oil

This is another reason to keep baking soda around, other than a fresh refrigerator. Mix an equal amount of baking soda with coconut oil. Spread it on your face, lightly rubbing. Leave on for about five minutes and rinse off with warm water. You are exfoliated and nourished.

Relaxation

One of my favorite projects when obtaining my holistic degree was preparing an original blend of essential oils in the aromatherapy course. I decided on an oil to support emotional concerns. This blend can serve to lift up the senses and spirit and help relieve the signs of the daily grind. The oils I used are known for their antidepressant qualities. I will share my formula for the blend, so you may find a sweet, relaxing moment during yoga, meditation, or just stillness. I love a waft of this to settle the senses and nerves. Namaste.

1 ounce (6 teaspoons) jojoba carrier oil (almond oil is another option)
4 drops bergamot
4 drops sandalwood
2 drops geranium

This blend can be used for massage or the bath. Another way to enjoy this would be dabbing a tissue and keeping it accessible in your purse or side of bed, to sniff for therapeutic effects. It will reduce stress. In the bath, it will act as a sleep aid. I use it in my pomander in certain rooms. When testing the scent, always sniff the cap lightly, or pass it by or around your nose. I also keep a bottle of ylang-ylang on my desk. A light pass by your nose, and it renders a quick lift of calm. Remember, not all senses are on the tongue, confirmed by the heavenly aroma of a freshly baked apple pie.

Acknowledgments

My grandparents, who had visions of a better life, boarded a steamship leaving Southern Italy to come to America in the early 1900s. They learned English, worked hard, became American citizens, and raised families, ultimately becoming part of the new growth of this great country.

My parents built their lives on the basis of our ancestors' values. They lived off the land and became self-sustaining, educated, and prosperous individuals. Ultimately, they led long, successful, happy, and healthy lives. They taught us many things and made sure we became ethical, honest, and compassionate adults to carry on their legacies into our lifetime. I miss them both every day and know they would be thrilled with this book, my labor of love and homage to their legacy.

My siblings, Joe, Lorraine, and Gina. I love you all, but we have had our differences, as all siblings do. In the end, we are all from the same gene pool and have an eternal connection built on the same principles. Of course, they also know their way around the kitchen and are great cooks. I am the middle child of five children. There is much to be said about that position in a family, especially when always wanting to keep the peace. At times, this is a very trying place to be. Regardless, we are stuck with each other. I never met my sister Loretta; she was our firstborn little girl and, sadly, passed away before I was born.

My friends and lovers. Thanks for being there, sharing my life and love, listening to my worries and discontent, and finally, enjoying lots of laughter and good times too. Also, thanks for loving my cooking and great parties. Without your encouragement and enjoying everything I served, I may have thought twice before writing *The Farmer's Daughter's Guide to Delicious and Nutritious Eating*.

Last but not least, my pets. Yes, I had a few and must mention them. I learned how to care for something other than myself at a young age. My first puppy was a toy fox terrier. Tino was his name. He lived for fifteen years and was the smartest, coolest little dog. He even understood Italian. We also had a beautiful collie, Flame. She was with us for many years and preferred running around the farm rather than being in the house. She was a true farm dog. We had many other pets, including cats, rabbits, and Dad's rare-breed pigeons. My father loved having different horses and ducks on our farm. He eventually became interested in thoroughbred racing with a successful history, as noted in a few photos in this book. My first pony was Shrimpy, a tiny dapple gray Shetland. Of course, Bamba, our pet deer, will always bring back fond memories. I realized that living in the country, you want to make everything your pet; it just seems natural. Ultimately, after completing this literary journey, I deeply long for that country lifestyle once again, and hopefully will be able to fulfill that desire.

About the Author

The happiness of others is my happiness.

The writing of *The Farmer's Daughter's Guide to Delicious and Nutritious Eating* has been one of the most challenging and emotionally provocative tasks I have ever pursued. Even with my education and career moves, businesses, and personal relationships, this project has taken me to a different level of consciousness in my memory, personal development, and life choices. It has been fulfilling. However, it was also a difficult emotional journey to travel back in time to remember and relive all the wonderful as well as sad events of my life, before I emerged to be the author of this book. Searching for all the family photos that are included in each chapter was such fun. I hope you enjoy them as much as I did finding them.

I steadily pursued my interests in natural medicine and holistic nutrition and am grateful for the opportunities that have come to me. I believe that healthy eating and healthy thinking works. I know that being more mindful in your thoughts, no matter what you are trying to accomplish, will give you a deeper perspective and eventually a more balanced outcome in your life.

I have learned that mindfulness matters most in how you perceive your life and the world around you. I am trying to not take myself so seriously, knowing that I am tested every day. After all my exploring, physically, emotionally, and intellectually, I have faith that the road I have traveled brought me to this moment and confirms that the choices I made were meant to be. My *destino*.

I hope you enjoyed *The Farmer's Daughter's Guide to Delicious and Nutritious Eating*. I am sure you have learned a little and smiled a lot, and maybe will be more thoughtful when buying or growing, cooking, serving, and enjoying food. Take the time to embrace the preparation, tasting, serving, and even the leftovers. Good food is a wonderful thing. It keeps us going. It makes our bodies speak to us, so pay attention. It brings people together to share a great meal or life experience. Food should be a pleasure for our eyes, our nose, and our palate. Thank you, and I wish you good health.

Mangiare sano e bene e godersi la vita!

Tanti baci a tutti,

Rosanne